SUPER SIMPLE BODY

INSIDE
THE
HEART

KARIN HALVORSON, M.D.
Consulting Editor, Diane Craig, M.A./Reading Specialist

A Division of ABDO
ABDO
Publishing Company

VISIT US AT WWW.ABDOPUBLISHING.COM

Published by ABDO Publishing Company, a division of
ABDO, P.O. Box 398166, Minneapolis, Minnesota 55439.
Copyright © 2013 by Abdo Consulting Group, Inc.
International copyrights reserved in all countries. No
part of this book may be reproduced in any form without
written permission from the publisher. Super SandCastle™
is a trademark and logo of ABDO Publishing Company.

Printed in the United States of America,
North Mankato, Minnesota
102012
012013

 PRINTED ON RECYCLED PAPER

Editor: Liz Salzmann
Content Developer: Nancy Tuminelly
Cover and Interior Design: Anders Hanson, Mighty Media
Photo Credits: Shutterstock, Dorling Kindersley RF/Thinkstock,
Colleen Dolphin

Library of Congress Cataloging-in-Publication Data
Halvorson, Karin, 1979-
  Inside the heart / Karin Halvorson, M.D. ; consulting editor, Diane
Craig, M.A./Reading Specialist.
    pages cm. -- (Super simple body)
  Audience: Age 4-10.
  ISBN 978-1-61783-612-1
  1. Heart--Physiology--Juvenile literature. I. Title.
  QP111.6.H35 2013
  612.17--dc23
                                2012030978

Super SandCastle™ books are created by a team of professional
educators, reading specialists, and content developers around five
essential components—phonemic awareness, phonics, vocabulary,
text comprehension, and fluency—to assist young readers as they
develop reading skills and strategies and increase their general
knowledge. All books are written, reviewed, and leveled for guided
reading, early reading intervention, and Accelerated Reader®
programs for use in shared, guided, and independent reading
and writing activities to support a balanced approach to literacy
instruction.

NOTE TO ADULTS

THIS BOOK is all about encouraging children to learn the science of how their bodies work! Be there to help make science fun and interesting for young readers. Many activities are included in this book to help children further explore what they've learned. Some require adult assistance and/or permission. Make sure children have appropriate places where they can do the activities safely.

Children may also have questions about what they've learned. Offer help and guidance when they have questions. Most of all encourage them to keep exploring and learning new things!

CONTENTS

YOUR BODY

YOUR HEART

You're amazing! So is your body!

Your body has a lot of different parts. Your eyes, ears, brain, stomach, lungs, and heart all work together every day. They keep you moving. Even when you don't realize it.

Your heart is a muscle. It works harder than any other muscle in your body. It makes sure all your cells have energy. That's not an easy job. You have more than 50 **trillion** cells in your body!

Your heart is near the center of your chest. Put your hand on the left side of your chest. You can feel your heart working!

ALL ABOUT THE

HEART

Your heart pumps your blood. The blood goes from your heart to every part of your body. Then it returns to your heart. That's called circulation.

{ FAST FACT }

AN ADULT HEART PUMPS ABOUT 1,900 GALLONS (7,200 L) OF BLOOD EVERY DAY!

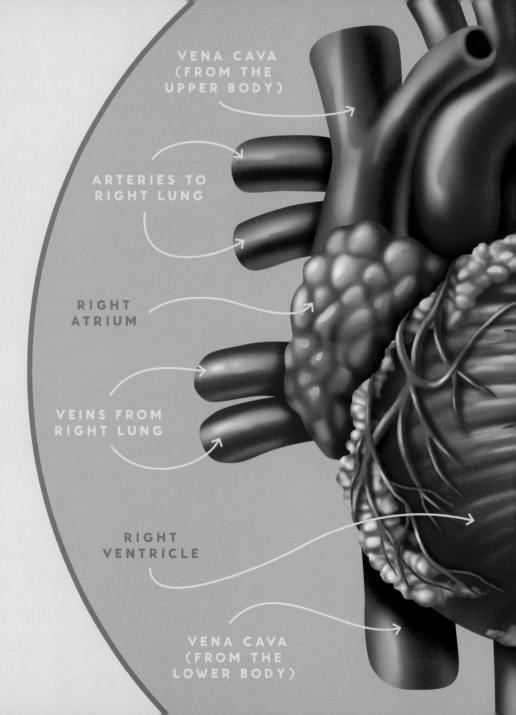

VENA CAVA (FROM THE UPPER BODY)

ARTERIES TO RIGHT LUNG

RIGHT ATRIUM

VEINS FROM RIGHT LUNG

RIGHT VENTRICLE

VENA CAVA (FROM THE LOWER BODY)

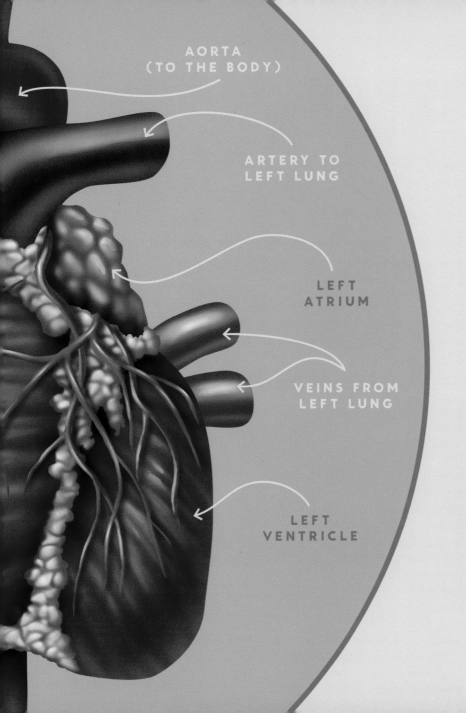

AORTA
(TO THE BODY)

ARTERY TO
LEFT LUNG

LEFT
ATRIUM

VEINS FROM
LEFT LUNG

LEFT
VENTRICLE

Blood travels through **blood vessels**.
It brings energy to your cells.

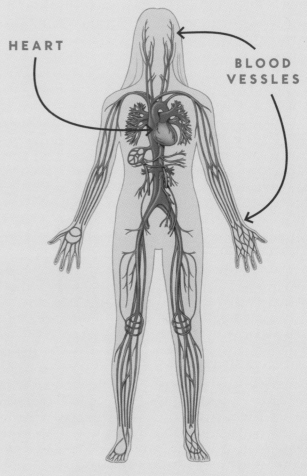

HEART

BLOOD
VESSLES

**BLOOD VESSELS REACH EVERY
PART OF YOUR BODY**

ENERGY

Everything runs on energy. Cars need gas. Lights need electricity. Your body needs energy too. It gets it from **nutrients** in food and air. Nutrients are chemicals that you need to live. Every time you eat or breathe, you bring nutrients into your body.

YOUR ENERGY COMES FROM FOOD AND AIR

Nutrients

Fats, proteins, and sugars are **nutrients**. They're in the food you eat. They give you energy.

Oxygen is a nutrient too. It's in the air you breathe. It helps your cells take energy from food. Without it, your cells would die.

When you eat and breathe, these nutrients go into your blood!

CIRCULATION

NATION

Your blood brings **nutrients** to your cells. It also carries away waste.

Blood goes through your **blood vessels**. Your blood vessels are like a highway system. They go all over your body.

Blood vessels that carry new blood away from the heart are called arteries.

Blood vessels that return used blood to the heart are called veins.

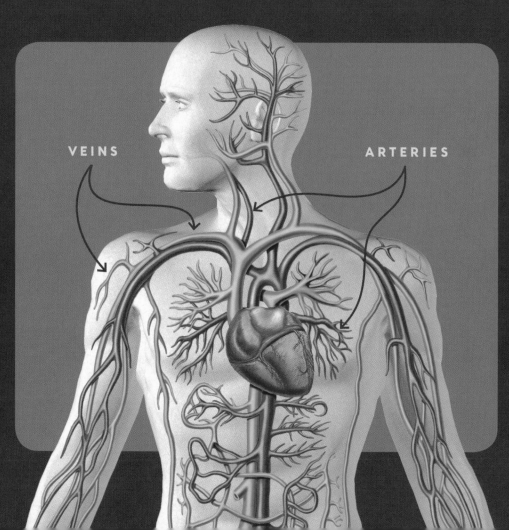

VEINS

ARTERIES

Your blood has special cells called blood cells.

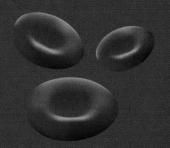

Red Blood Cells

Red blood cells are the most common blood cells. They carry oxygen.

White Blood Cells

White blood cells help keep your body healthy. They fight off **germs**.

Platelets

Platelets help heal you. They stop the bleeding when you get a cut.

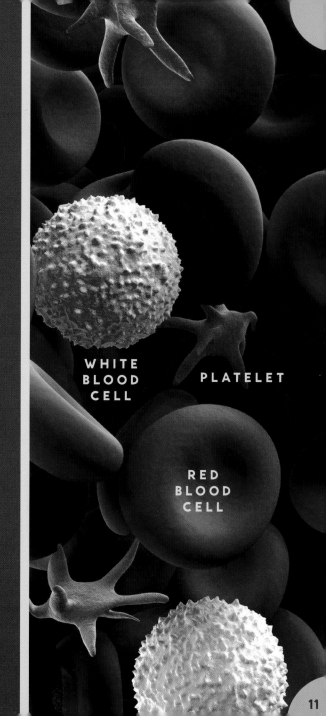

WHITE BLOOD CELL

PLATELET

RED BLOOD CELL

TWO SIDES

TO EVERY HEART

Your heart has two sides. They are the left heart and the right heart. Each side acts like a pump.

Your veins bring used blood to your right heart. It pumps the blood into your lungs. Your lungs renew the blood by adding oxygen.

Your left heart takes the new blood from your lungs. It pumps the blood out to your body through your arteries.

You can hear the sound of your heart pumping. It's called your heartbeat. LUB-DUB, LUB-DUB!

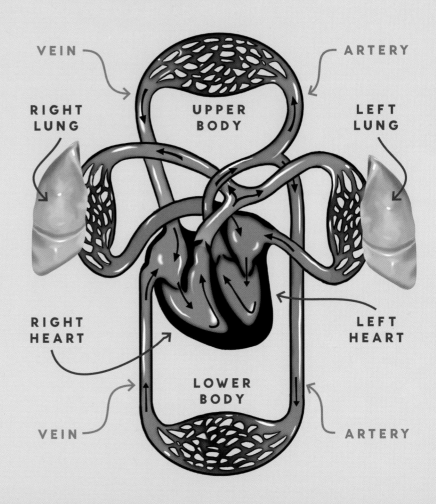

VEIN

ARTERY

RIGHT LUNG

UPPER BODY

LEFT LUNG

RIGHT HEART

LEFT HEART

LOWER BODY

VEIN

ARTERY

PARTS

Each side of your heart has a top part and a bottom part. The top part is called the atrium (AY-TREE-UHM). The bottom part is called the ventricle (VEN-TRI-KUHL).

Blood enters the atriums. When they fill up, they release the blood. It flows through **valves** into the ventricles. Then the ventricles **squeeze** it out.

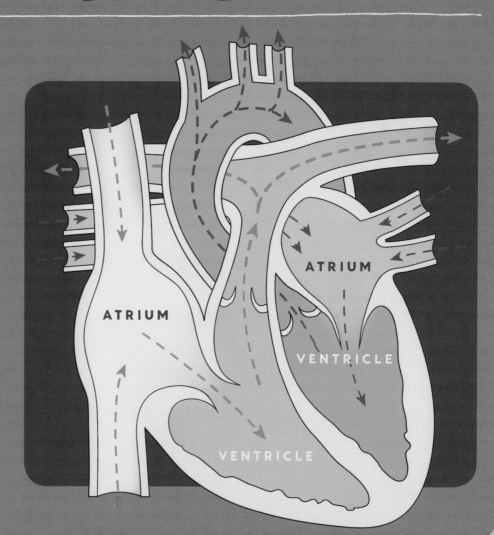

ATRIUM

ATRIUM

VENTRICLE

VENTRICLE

WE'VE GOT THE BEAT!

HEAR YOUR HEARTBEAT!

WHAT YOU NEED: SMALL FUNNEL, 60 CM (200 MM) OF RUBBER TUBING, TAPE, STOPWATCH

HOW TO DO IT

1 Put one end of the tube into the funnel.

2 Put tape around the end of the funnel to hold it to the tube.

3 Put the funnel over your chest. Hold the other end up to your ear. Be careful not to put it in your ear! Can you hear a thumping that sounds like "lub-dub"? That's your heartbeat!

4 Find your heart rate. It's the number of times your heart beats in a minute. Start the stopwatch. Count your heartbeats. Stop counting at 15 seconds. Then multiply that number by four. That's your heart rate.

WHAT'S HAPPENING?

Your heart makes noise when it pumps your blood. The funnel and tube help you hear the sound better. It's like a doctor's **stethoscope**.

ONE WAY
ONLY

Each part of your heart is like a room. Your blood goes through a valve to get from one room to the next.

A valve is a like a one-way door. It keeps your blood from flowing backward. After the blood goes through, the door closes.

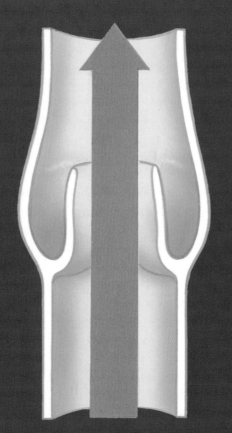

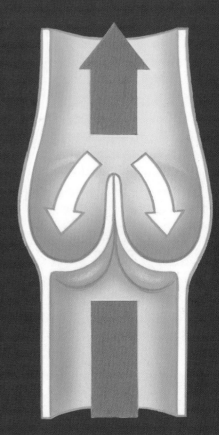

OPEN VALVE   CLOSED VALVE

Your heart has four valves.

The tricuspid and pulmonic valves are on the right side. The tricuspid valve separates the atrium from the ventricle. Blood goes to the lungs through the pulmonic valve.

The mitral and aortic valves are on the left side. The mitral valve divides the atrium and the ventricle. The blood goes out to the body through the aortic valve.

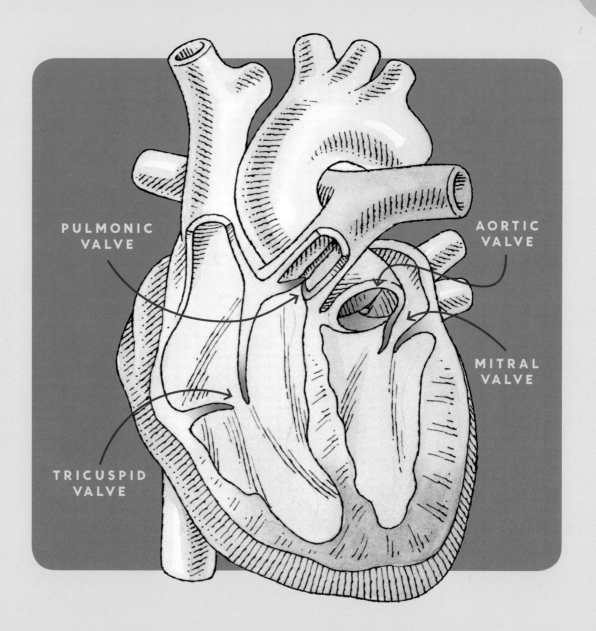

PULMONIC VALVE

AORTIC VALVE

MITRAL VALVE

TRICUSPID VALVE

VALUABLE VALVES

MAKE A HEART VALVE!

WHAT YOU NEED: CARDBOARD TUBE, DUCT TAPE, PAPER, RULER, PENCIL, GLUE, SCISSORS, CLEAR TAPE

HOW TO DO IT

1 Cover the tube with duct tape. Don't cover the ends.

2 Draw two 3-inch (7.5 cm) circles on paper. Cut them out. Poke a hole in the center of each one with a pencil. Make small cuts around the edge of each circle. They should be .5 inches (1.2 cm) long.

3 Put glue on one side of each circle. Place one circle over each end of the tube. Press the small flaps onto the side of the tube.

4 Blow into one end of the tube. Then suck in air. Did the air flow easily? Cut out a square of paper. Put it over the hole in one end. Tape just one edge of the square. Blow into the other end of the tube. Then suck air in. Does the air move as easily as it did before?

WHAT'S HAPPENING?

It is harder to suck air in with the paper over the hole. The paper is like the valves in your heart. The valves keep blood from going the wrong way.

THE LEFT HEART

When blood leaves your lungs, it is full of oxygen. It flows from the lungs into the left heart.

The blood enters the atrium. Then it flows into the ventricle. The ventricle pumps it into a large artery. This artery is called the aorta (AY-OR-TUH).

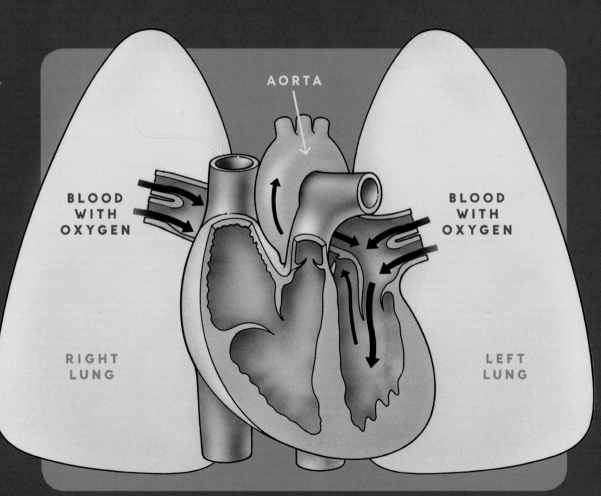

AORTA

BLOOD WITH OXYGEN

BLOOD WITH OXYGEN

RIGHT LUNG

LEFT LUNG

ARTERIES

Arteries take new blood from your heart to the rest of your body. Some go up to your head. Others go all the way down to your toes!

The aorta is the biggest artery. The other arteries branch off from it. They get smaller and smaller. They are like branches on a tree.

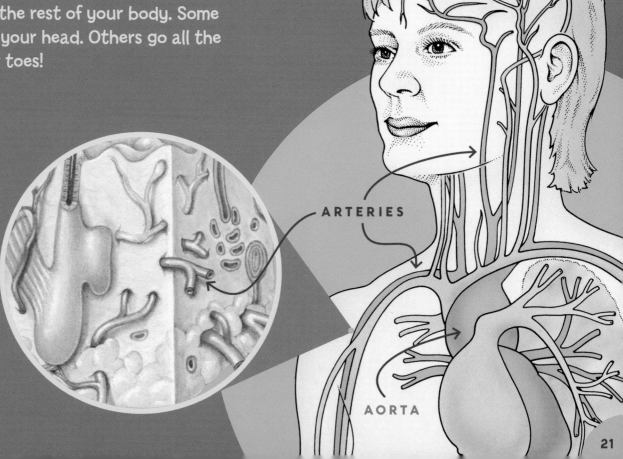

ARTERIES

AORTA

PUMP ▶ IT UP!

MAKE A HEART PUMP!

WHAT YOU NEED: WIDEMOUTHED JAR, WATER, BALLOON, SCISSORS, RUBBER BAND, PENCIL, STRAW, LARGE BOWL

HOW TO DO IT

1. Fill the jar half way with water.

2. Cut off the stem of the balloon.

3. Stretch the rest of the balloon over the top of the jar. Put the rubber band around the edge to hold it tight.

4. Use the pencil to poke a hole in the balloon.

5. Put the straw through the hole.

6. Put the jar in the bowl. Push on the balloon with your finger. Watch what happens!

WHAT'S HAPPENING?

Your finger is like the pumping of the heart. Water is pushed up through the straw. This is like blood pumping through your aorta.

CAPILLARIES

Your arteries carry new blood to your capillaries. Capillaries are the smallest blood vessels. They connect your arteries to your veins.

FAST FACT

CAPILLARIES ARE ONLY ONE CELL WIDE!

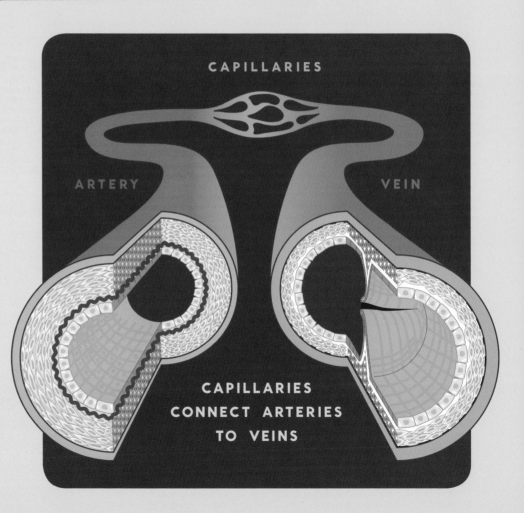

CAPILLARIES

ARTERY

VEIN

CAPILLARIES CONNECT ARTERIES TO VEINS

The capillaries pass **nutrients** in the blood to your cells. Oxygen, fat, sugar, and protein are important nutrients. Your cells use them for energy.

When cells make energy, they also create waste. **Carbon dioxide** is one type of waste. Your capillaries take the waste from your cells. They put the waste in your blood. Then the used blood goes into your veins.

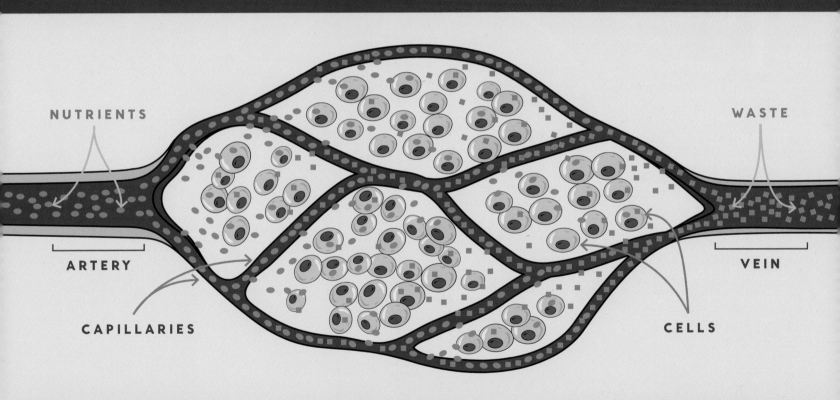

NUTRIENTS

WASTE

ARTERY

VEIN

CAPILLARIES

CELLS

CAPILLARIES DROP OFF NUTRIENTS AND PICK UP WASTE

VEINS

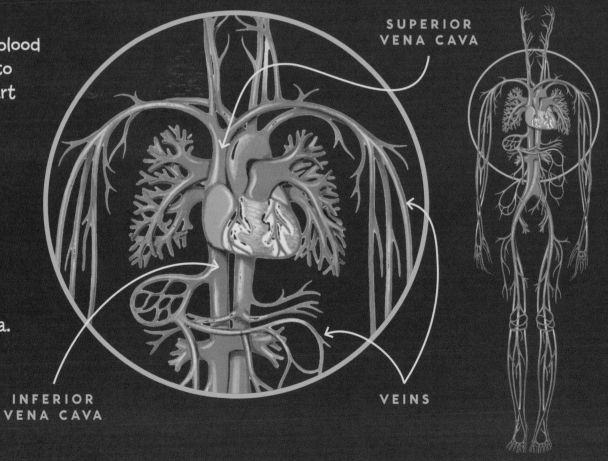

The used blood returns to your heart through your veins. It goes through larger and larger veins.

The two biggest veins are the superior vena cava and the inferior vena cava.

SUPERIOR
VENA CAVA

INFERIOR
VENA CAVA

VEINS

Superior Vena Cava

The superior vena cava carries blood from your upper body.

Inferior Vena Cava

The inferior vena cava brings blood up from your lower body.

Both veins lead to the right heart.

ATRIUM

RIGHT HEART

LEFT HEART

VENTRICLE

INFERIOR
VENA CAVA

THE RIGHT HEART

U sed blood returns to the right heart. It falls from the atrium into the ventricle. The ventricle pumps it to your lungs.

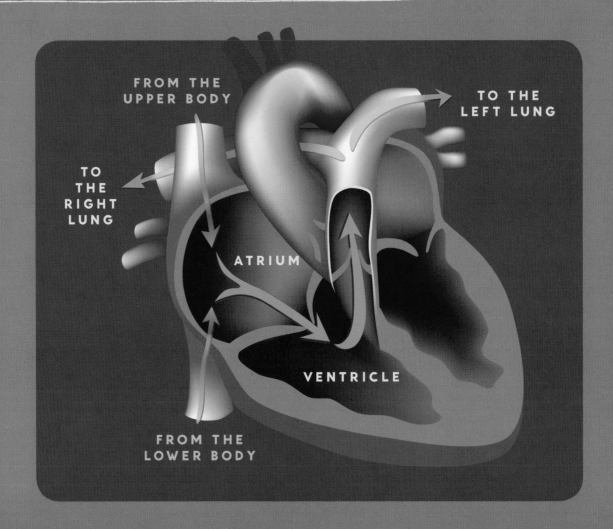

FROM THE UPPER BODY

TO THE LEFT LUNG

TO THE RIGHT LUNG

ATRIUM

VENTRICLE

FROM THE LOWER BODY

Your lungs remove **carbon dioxide** from your blood. You get rid of carbon dioxide every time you breathe out.

Your lungs also add oxygen to your blood. That makes it new again!

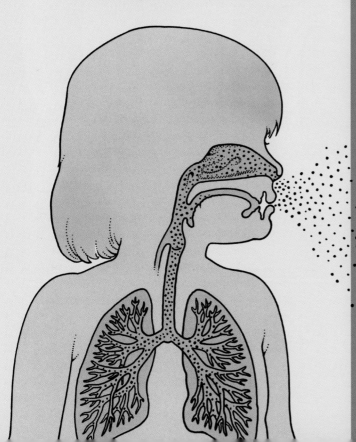

HEART HAPPY

Most people are born with healthy hearts. It's important to keep yours in good shape!

EXERCISE! Your heart is a muscle. You want it to be strong. Do something active every day.

EAT HEALTHY! Your body needs healthy food. Eat fresh fruits and veggies every day.

DON'T SMOKE! Ask the people around you not to smoke. Smoke is bad for your heart and blood vessels.

HEART ♥ WORK

SEE HOW YOUR HEART WORKS!

WHAT YOU NEED: BALLOON, SCISSORS, HOT WATER BOTTLE, RED FOOD COLORING, RUBBER BAND, WOODEN SKEWER, RUBBER TUBE, BOWL

HOW TO DO IT

1 Cut the stem off the balloon.

2 If the hot water bottle has a neck, fold it down. Fill the bottle half way with water. Add ten drops of red food coloring. This is the heart and the blood.

3 Stretch the balloon over the opening of the hot water bottle. Use a rubber band to hold it in place. Then poke a hole in the balloon with the skewer. The balloon is a valve.

4 Push the rubber tube through the hole in the balloon. Make sure it goes pretty far into the bottle.

5 Put the other end of the tube in the bowl. **Squeeze** the hot water bottle. Watch as the blood comes out.

WHAT'S HAPPENING?

Your hand pumps your heart. The blood flows out and into the bowl.

GLOSSARY

CARBON DIOXIDE - a gas mainly produced in the bodies of people and animals, which becomes part of the air they breathe out.

GERM - a tiny, living organism that can make people sick.

NUTRIENT - something that helps living things grow. Vitamins, minerals, and proteins are nutrients.

SQUEEZE - to press or grip something tightly.

STETHOSCOPE - a medical device used to listen to sounds inside the body.

TRILLION - a very large number. One trillion is also written 1,000,000,000,000.